AGATHA CHRISTIE,
WOMAN OF MYSTERY

Many people enjoy reading murder .... se
they are puzzles. C. ...... e
before the detective t ...... s
the broken chair an a ......)
How did the murder ......
she) have a key? Why ...... ee coffee cups on
the table?

Agatha Christie's murder mysteries are famous all over
the world. She wrote more than seventy books and they
have sold millions of copies. There have been many
television plays and films of her stories. Her detectives,
Hercule Poirot and Miss Marple, are famous too – a
short round Belgian with a black moustache, and a dear
little old lady, who sees, hears, and remembers
everything.

This is a story about Agatha Christie's life. What kind
of person was she? How much do we know about her?
She was rich, famous, and twice married. And there
was a mystery in her life, too . . .

OXFORD BOOKWORMS LIBRARY

True Stories

Agatha Christie, Woman of Mystery

Stage 2 (700 headwords)

Series Editor: Jennifer Bassett
Founder Editor: Tricia Hedge
Activities Editors: Jennifer Bassett and Alison Baxter

JOHN ESCOTT

Agatha Christie, Woman of Mystery

OXFORD UNIVERSITY PRESS

OXFORD
UNIVERSITY PRESS

Great Clarendon Street, Oxford OX2 6DP

Oxford University Press is a department of the University of Oxford.
It furthers the University's objective of excellence in research, scholarship,
and education by publishing worldwide in

Oxford New York

Auckland Cape Town Dar es Salaam Hong Kong Karachi
Kuala Lumpur Madrid Melbourne Mexico City Nairobi
New Delhi Shanghai Taipei Toronto

With offices in

Argentina Austria Brazil Chile Czech Republic France Greece
Guatemala Hungary Italy Japan Poland Portugal Singapore
South Korea Switzerland Thailand Turkey Ukraine Vietnam

OXFORD and OXFORD ENGLISH are registered trade marks of
Oxford University Press in the UK and in certain other countries

ISBN 978 0 19 479050 5

A complete recording of this Bookworms edition of
Agatha Christie, Woman of Mystery is available on audio CD ISBN 978 0 19 478973 8

Printed in China

ACKNOWLEDGEMENTS

The publishers would like to thank the following
for their kind permission to reproduce photographs:
British Film Institute p 21; Hulton Getty Picture Collection Ltd
pp 4, 17 (V Doone/Dartmoor), 25, 40; Mander and Mitchenson Theatre
Collection Ltd pp 26, 29, 38; Popperfoto p 35; The Ronald Grant Archive
pp 32, 36; Topham Picturepoint pp 10, 13
Illustrated by: Nick Hardcastle

Word count (main text): 5955 words

For more information on the Oxford Bookworms Library,
visit www.oup.com/bookworms

CONTENTS

—

CHAPTER 1

'Why don't you write a story?'

Agatha Mary Clarissa Miller was bored. It was a winter morning in 1908, and she was in bed because she was ill.

'I'm feeling much better today,' she said to her mother, Clara. 'I think I'll get up.'

'You're still ill,' said Clara. 'The doctor told you to stay in bed and keep warm. And that's what you're going to do!'

Agatha was eighteen years old at this time, but in those days daughters had to do what their mothers told them.

'But I'm *bored*!'

'Well, do something, then,' said her mother. 'Read a book. Or write a story. Yes, why don't you write a story?'

'Write a story?' said Agatha, surprised.

'Yes,' her mother said. 'Like Madge.'

Madge was Agatha's sister. She was eleven years older

than Agatha, and sometimes wrote short stories for magazines like *Vanity Fair*.

'I don't think that I can write stories,' said Agatha.

'How do you know?' said her mother. 'You've never tried.' And she went to find a pencil and paper.

Soon after, Agatha sat up in bed and began to write a story. It was called *House of Beauty*, a strange story about dreams.

It wasn't a very good story. She typed it on Madge's old typewriter, and sent it off to a magazine. But they sent it back with a letter: *Thank you for sending us your story. We are afraid we cannot publish it ...*

'You must try again,' said her mother. Clara was always sure that her daughters could do anything.

So Agatha went on writing stories, and sending them out to magazines – but they all came back. She was a little disappointed.

'I'll try writing a novel,' she decided.

An idea came to her. She remembered seeing a beautiful young girl in a hotel in Cairo when she was visiting Egypt with Clara. The girl was always with two men, one on each side of her. One day, Agatha heard someone say, 'That girl will have to decide between them some time.'

It was all that Agatha needed for an idea, and she began writing. It was not a detective novel. It was the story of a young girl who lived in Cairo, and it was called *Snow Upon the Desert.* It was really two long stories put together to make a book. When it was finished, Agatha sent it to three or four publishers, but they all sent it back.

'Oh dear,' said Agatha. 'What shall I do now?'

'Why don't you show it to Eden Phillpotts?' said Clara.

Eden Phillpotts was a writer who lived near the Millers. During his life, he wrote more than a hundred popular

An idea for a novel . . .

novels, and many plays for the theatre. Agatha was a little afraid of sending her novel to this famous man, but she agreed to do it and sent it off.

Mr Phillpotts was a good writer, and also a kind man. He read Agatha's novel carefully and wrote her a letter.

Some of your writing is very good, so I am sending you a letter to take to my agent, Hughes Massie …

Agatha – still only eighteen years old – went to London

Torquay in the early 1900s

on the train. It was a long journey – more than 200 miles from her home in Torquay in Devon, and the trains were not so fast in those days.

She was very shy, and Hughes Massie was a big, frightening man. Agatha gave him the letter from Eden Phillpotts. Massie read it, talked with Agatha for a while, then kept her book to read.

Agatha went home to wait.

Some months later, Massie returned *Snow Upon the Desert* to her. *I do not think that I can find a publisher for it,* he wrote to her. *The best thing is to stop thinking about it any more and to write another book.*

Agatha was disappointed. She did write another book, but some other important things happened in her life first.

CHAPTER 2

———

A shy young man

Agatha's father, Frederick, died in 1901, when Agatha was eleven years old. He was an American, and was ten years older than Clara. After he died, Clara began to travel a lot, and often took Agatha with her.

In 1911, when Agatha was twenty-one, Clara was ill.

'You need to go somewhere warm and sunny to get better,' Clara's doctor told her.

So Clara decided to go to Egypt again, and she took Agatha with her. They stayed in a hotel in Cairo. There were some English soldiers staying near the hotel, and they often came to the hotel dances.

Agatha was a shy young woman, but she loved to dance. During her stay in Cairo, she went to fifty dances. She met a lot of exciting young men and had a wonderful time.

When she came back to England, she was soon getting invitations to garden parties, tennis parties, dances, and to country houses for the weekend.

Then a young army officer called Reggie Lucy came home from Hong Kong. Agatha was a friend of Reggie's three sisters, and often played tennis with them. But she did not know Reggie. He was a very shy young man who did not go out very much. He liked to play golf but did not like parties or dances.

'I like to play golf, but I'm not very good at it,' Agatha said when she met him.

'I – I could help you,' said Reggie, shyly. He had dark hair and brown eyes. Agatha liked him.

So, while Reggie was in England, he and Agatha played golf nearly every day.

One very warm day they played golf for a little while, then Agatha said, 'I'm hot, Reggie! Shall we have a rest?'

They sat under a tree, out of the sun, and talked. Then, suddenly, Reggie said, 'I want to marry you, Agatha. Did

Reggie and Agatha played golf nearly every day.

you know that? Perhaps you did. But you are still very young, and—'

'No, I'm not!' said Agatha. 'Not very young.'

'Of course, a pretty girl like you could marry anybody,' said Reggie.

'I don't think I want to marry *anybody*,' Agatha said. 'I – yes, I think I'd like to marry you!'

'I have to go back to Hong Kong in ten days' time,' said Reggie. 'And I'll be there for two years, But when I come back, if there isn't anybody . . .'

'There won't be anybody,' said Agatha.

So Reggie went back to Hong Kong.

Agatha wrote letters to him, and he wrote to her. It was all agreed. When Reggie came home again, they would get married.

CHAPTER 3

Tea at the railway station

On October the 12th, 1912, when Agatha was twenty-two, she went to a dance at the home of Lord and Lady Clifford. They lived near Chudleigh, twelve miles from Torquay, and there were many young people there for Agatha to talk to.

During the evening a young army officer came up to her.

'Will you dance with me?' he asked Agatha.

'Me?' said Agatha. 'Oh, yes, all right.'

He was tall and good-looking, with friendly blue eyes, and his name was Archibald Christie. Agatha liked him immediately. They danced together many times that evening, and Archie told her his plans.

'I want to fly,' he said, 'and I'm trying to get into the Royal Flying Corps.'

'How exciting!' said Agatha.

A week later, she was having tea with some friends at a house opposite Ashfield, her home, when there was a telephone call for her. It was her mother.

'Come home, will you, Agatha?' said Clara. 'There's a

Archibald and Agatha danced together many times that evening.

young man here. He's just arrived and I'm giving him tea. I don't know him, and I think he wants to see you.'

Agatha had to leave her friends and hurry home, so she was not very pleased. But when she got home, she found Archie Christie waiting for her.

'Hello,' he said. 'I was in

Agatha as a young woman

Torquay and – and I thought that perhaps it would be nice to see you.' His face was red and he looked at his shoes.

Agatha smiled.

Archie stayed for the rest of the afternoon, and for supper that evening. When it was time for him to leave, he said, 'Will you come to a concert in Exeter with me, Agatha? We can go to the Redcliffe Hotel for tea after the concert.'

'I'd love to,' said Agatha, then looked at Clara. 'Can I, mother?'

'A concert, yes, Agatha,' said Clara. 'But tea at a hotel? No, I don't think so. Not a *hotel*.'

'Perhaps I could take Agatha to tea in – in the restaurant at Exeter railway station!' said Archie.

Agatha tried not to smile, but her mother agreed. So Agatha and Archie went to the concert – and then had tea at Exeter railway station!

'There's a New Year's dance in Torquay on the second of January,' said Agatha, when Archie took her home later. 'Will you come?'

He smiled. 'Of course,' he said. 'I want to see you as often as I can.'

But when Archie came to the New Year's dance he was very quiet and did not seem happy. He seemed to be worried about something, but Agatha said nothing. Two days later, on the 4th of January, 1913, they went to another concert together. Archie was still very quiet, and after the concert Agatha asked, 'What's wrong, Archie?'

'The Royal Flying Corps have said "yes" to me,' said Archie. 'I have to leave Exeter in two days' time. I have to go to Salisbury.' He looked at her. 'Agatha, you've *got* to marry me! There will never be anyone for me, only you! I've known that since our first evening together, at the Cliffords' dance.'

Agatha was very surprised. 'But – but I can't marry you. I've already told Reggie that I'll marry him.' And then she told him about Reggie Lucy.

'You didn't marry him before he went away,' said Archie. 'Why not? It's because you don't really love him!'

'We thought it was better to wait—' began Agatha.

'I won't wait,' said Archie. 'I want to marry you next month, or the month after.'

'We can't!' said Agatha. 'We haven't got any money. How will we live?'

But she did want to marry Archie.

'Archie has asked me to marry him, and I want to. I want to very much!' she told her mother.

Clara was very surprised. 'You must wait,' she told them both. 'I like you, Archie, but you are only twenty-three years old, and neither of you has any money.'

So Archie went to Salisbury, and he and Agatha waited. Agatha wrote to Reggie Lucy. It was a difficult letter to write, but Reggie wrote a very kind letter back to her. 'Don't worry about it,' he told her. 'I understand.'

* * *

In August 1914, England was suddenly at war with Germany. Archie went to France with the Royal Flying Corps, and Agatha went to work as a volunteer nurse at the Torbay Hospital in Torquay.

Archie came back to England for five days in December,

and Agatha went up to London to meet him. Then the two of them went down to Bristol, where Archie's mother lived. They could not wait any longer. They wanted to get married.

Archie's mother was not happy about this, but Clara thought differently. 'Yes, get married now,' she said. 'There's a war on. Who knows what will happen? Be happy while you can.'

So Agatha and Archie were married at last on the 24th of December, 1914. Two days later, Archie went back to the war, and Agatha did not see him again for six months.

* * *

Archibald Christie

During the summer of 1915, Agatha was ill and could not do any nursing work at the hospital for three or four weeks. Then, when she returned, she went to work in the hospital dispensary. And here she learned something which was very useful for a writer of detective stories. She learned about poisons.

CHAPTER 4

A detective story

One day, some time before the war, Agatha was talking with her sister, Madge, about detective stories. They both enjoyed reading this kind of book very much.

'I'd like to try and write a detective story myself,' said Agatha.

'You couldn't do it,' said Madge. 'They're very difficult to do. I've thought about it.'

'Well, one day I'm going to try,' said Agatha.

The idea stayed in Agatha's head, and she wanted to show Madge that she could do it. And when, years later, she went to work in the hospital dispensary, she again began to think about writing a detective story.

'There must be a murder in it, of course,' she thought. The questions ran busily around inside her head. 'But what kind of murder? A death by poisoning? Who will die? Who

In the hospital dispensary Agatha learned about poisons.

will the murderer be? When? How? Why? Where? And what about a detective?'

There were some Belgian people living in Torquay, who were there because of the war in Belgium. Clara, like everyone in the town, was very kind and helpful to them when they arrived. She gave them chairs and beds for their homes, and tried to make them feel happy and comfortable. Now, Agatha suddenly remembered them.

'What about a Belgian detective?' she thought, and began to build the character in her head. 'He'll be a very clever, very tidy little man. But what shall I call him? I know, I'll call him Hercules!' She smiled. 'It's a good name

15

for a small man. And his second name? Poirot. Hercules –
no, Hercule Poirot! Yes, that's it.'

Agatha thought about her detective story during every
quiet minute in the dispensary. She knew a lot about
poisons now. She knew which poisons worked quickly,
and which worked slowly. She knew how much to give,
and what different poisons smelt and tasted like. She knew
how people died from poisons – did their faces turn blue?
Did they die in their sleep, or die screaming in pain? A good
detective – and a good writer of detective stories – must
know these things. She began to write her story at home,
and used Madge's old typewriter again.

'What are you doing?' Clara asked her one day.

'I'm writing a detective novel,' said Agatha, 'I want to
finish it, but it's very difficult.'

'Why don't you finish it during your holiday?' said
Clara. 'Go away somewhere nice and quiet, and take it
with you. Where do you want to go? Dartmoor?'

'Yes!' said Agatha. 'Dartmoor!'

Dartmoor was a beautiful, lonely moor in Devon.
Agatha took Madge's typewriter with her and stayed at the
Moorland Hotel at Hay Tor. It was a large hotel with a lot
of rooms, but not many people were staying there. For two
weeks she wrote in her room every morning, then went for
long walks alone on the moor in the afternoons. Everything
went well. The characters seemed to come alive inside her

Dartmoor, a beautiful, lonely moor in Devon

head, and during her walks she planned her writing for the next day.

She finished the last half of the book during her holiday, and soon after she sent it to a publisher. They returned it, but Agatha was not surprised. She sent it out again, but it came back once more. She sent it to a third publisher, but they returned it, too. Then she sent it to The Bodley Head publishing company – and forgot all about it.

Two years went by. Archie came back to work in London, the war ended, and Agatha had a baby – Rosalind. The three of them were living in a flat in London when a letter arrived one morning in 1919.

It was from The Bodley Head. Agatha quickly opened the letter, and saw the words:

... will you call at our offices? ... we would like to talk about your book ...

'It's about my book – *The Mysterious Affair at Styles,*' she told Archie. 'I think they want to publish it!'

'Then you must go and see them at once!' said Archie.

Agatha went to the publishers' office. She met John Lane, a small man with white hair.

'Do sit down,' he said. He had a kind voice, and blue eyes that looked carefully at Agatha. 'Some of my readers think that we could publish your book. But you will need to change the last chapter. And there are a few other small things ...'

Agatha was too excited to listen. She was happy to do anything. *The Mysterious Affair at Styles* was her first detective story, and she wanted to see it in the bookshops. So she wrote a different ending for it and changed one or two more small things, and at last John Lane was pleased with it.

CHAPTER 5

———

A good detective-story writer

Agatha's first book, *The Mysterious Affair at Styles,* was published in 1920. But before this, she began writing another book.

It was Archie's idea.

'Mother is finding it difficult to pay all the bills at Ashfield,' Agatha told him.

'Why doesn't she sell Ashfield?' Archie said to Agatha. 'The house is too big for just one person. Then she can buy something smaller.'

'Sell Ashfield?' said Agatha. 'Oh, no! She can't! I love it – and it's our family home.'

'Then why don't *you* do something about it?' said Archie.

'Do something? What do you mean?'

'Why don't you write another book?' said Archie. 'Perhaps it will make a lot of money.'

Agatha thought about it. Ashfield was her family home, and it must stay in the family. Could she do anything to help?

'Perhaps I *could* write another book,' she thought. 'But what can it be about?'

The answer came one day when she was having tea in a

tea-shop. Two people were talking at a table near her. Agatha heard a name – and began to listen. They were talking about somebody called Jane Fish.

'What a strange name,' thought Agatha. 'But what a good beginning for a story! Somebody hears a strange name in a tea-shop. And then . . . ? Wait, perhaps "Jane Finn" will be better. Yes! Now, let me think . . . '

And before Agatha left the tea-shop, an idea for a story was running around inside her head. She went home and began it immediately.

She called it *The Secret Adversary*, and the book was published in 1922.

The story did not have the Belgian detective Hercule Poirot in it, but her next book, *Murder on the Links*, did. Readers loved Poirot. He was a very short, tidy little man, with green eyes, black hair, and a beautiful black moustache. And, like another famous detective, Sherlock Holmes, he was very, very clever. He was not shy about this, and was always telling other characters in the story just how clever he was.

Other books followed, some with Poirot, some without – *The Man in the Brown Suit*, *Poirot Investigates*, and *The Secret of Chimneys*.

Hughes Massie, the agent, was helping Agatha now. 'You need another publisher,' he told her. 'A publisher who will pay you more than The Bodley Head. You're a

Hercule Poirot, played by the actor David Suchet

good detective-story writer, Agatha, and your books are beginning to sell well.'

So Massie sent Agatha's next book – *The Murder of Roger Ackroyd* – to William Collins' publishers. It was an important book for Agatha.

The Murder of Roger Ackroyd came out in the spring of 1926 – and people began to talk about it immediately.

What did they talk about? The big surprise at the end of the book!

'That's cheating!' some people said, when they got to the end and found out the name of the murderer.

'No, it's not,' said other readers. 'It's a very clever story.'

'What's the matter with everybody?' Agatha said to Archie. 'I didn't cheat. It's wrong to say that. People must read the story carefully.'

And she was right. All the clues *were* there in the story, and a very clever reader *could* guess the name of the murderer. But most people couldn't.

(So what was the surprise at the end, and who was the murderer? The only way to find out is to read the book!)

After *The Murder of Roger Ackroyd* was published, more and more people began to buy Agatha's books, and Agatha had more money to spend.

The Christies bought a house at Sunningdale, about thirty miles from London.

'What shall we call it?' said Agatha.

'Styles,' said Archie, 'after your first book.'

And they put a picture of the front cover of the book, *The Mysterious Affair at Styles*, on the wall.

But not long after they moved to Sunningdale, something happened that put Agatha's name on the front pages of every newspaper in England.

She disappeared.

People think that it happened because she was very unhappy at this time. First, her mother died. And then Agatha found out that Archie was in love with a young woman called Nancy Neele.

CHAPTER 6

Agatha disappears

On the morning of Friday, the 3rd of December, 1926, Archie left Styles and went to stay with some friends for the weekend. Nancy Neele was also staying at this house for the weekend. Perhaps Agatha knew this, perhaps she didn't – we can't be sure.

Nobody knows what Agatha was thinking, late that dark winter evening. Rosalind, now seven years old, was in bed. The Christies' two housemaids were in the kitchen. But we know this. At about eleven o'clock that evening, Agatha went out and drove away in her car.

She did not return home that night.

* * *

On Saturday morning, a woman arrived by taxi at the Hydro Hotel in Harrogate, Yorkshire. The Hydro was one of Harrogate's biggest and best hotels, near the centre of the town.

'Can I have a room, please?' the woman asked. She was

carrying a small suitcase, and she looked very tired.

'Yes, of course,' said the man behind the hotel desk. 'There's a nice room on the first floor – room number five. It has hot and cold water, and the cost is seven pounds for a week.'

'Thank you, that will be all right,' said the woman.

'What name, please?' asked the man.

'Mrs Teresa Neele,' said the woman with the suitcase.

* * *

Also on that cold Saturday morning in December, a fifteen-year-old boy was walking beside a lake called the Silent Pool. This was at a place called Newlands Corner, about fourteen miles from Sunningdale. The boy's name was George Best.

Suddenly, George saw a car. It was off the road, down by the lake, but the lights were on.

'That's strange,' he thought. 'Why is that car down there, and why are the lights on?' And he went to have a better look.

The car was empty, but the driver's door was open. George looked inside. He saw a coat, and an open suitcase. Half-out of the suitcase were three dresses, some shoes – and some papers with the name 'Mrs Agatha Christie' on them.

George quickly went to find a policeman.

* * *

Agatha's car, found at Newlands Corner

The newspapers were soon full of the story, and Agatha's picture was on the front pages. Where was the detective-story writer? Was she dead? Was she murdered? Did she kill herself?

The *Daily News* wanted answers to these questions, and said, on December the 7th, that it would give £100 to the first person with the answers. By the next weekend, hundreds of policemen and thousands of people were looking for her.

'Did your wife ever talk about disappearing?' a *Daily Mail* reporter asked Archie.

'Yes,' said Archie. 'She once told her sister, "I could disappear any time I wanted to. I would plan it carefully,

NEWS, TUESDAY, DECEMBER 7, 1926.

£100 REWARD.

WHERE IS MRS. CHRISTIE?

SEARCH FOR MISSING NOVELIST.

'DAILY NEWS' OFFER.

The "Daily News" offers £100 reward to the first person furnishing us with information leading to the discovery of the whereabouts, if alive, of Mrs. Christie.

MRS. AGATHA CHRISTIE.

...stries by the police, however, have ...the address at which

Did Agatha plan to disappear? Did she change how she looked?
On 11th December the Daily News *showed two pictures*
(above, left and right) of Agatha Christie with different hair
and wearing glasses.

and nobody would find me." Perhaps this happened. Or perhaps she's ill and can't remember who she is.'

The police asked Archie lots of questions, watched his house, and followed him to his office.

'They think I've murdered Agatha,' he told a friend.

*   *   *

The woman at the Hydro Hotel had breakfast in her room each morning, and sat quietly reading in the hotel sitting-room in the afternoons. She said 'Good morning' and 'Good afternoon' to other people in the hotel, and seemed worried because there were no letters for her.

But one of the chambermaids went to see Mrs Taylor, the wife of the hotel manager.

'Mrs Neele looks like the woman in the *Daily Mail* picture,' said the chambermaid. 'You know the one – Agatha Christie!'

Mrs Taylor spoke to her husband about it, but they decided to say nothing. They did not want any trouble at the hotel.

But two more people at the Hydro Hotel were also looking carefully at 'Mrs Teresa Neele'.

Bob Tappin and Bob Leeming played music in the hotel each evening, and both of them watched the quiet woman in the corner of the room – and began to think.

'I'm sure that Neele woman is Agatha Christie,' Bob Tappin said to his friend one evening.

'I think you're right,' Bob Leeming agreed. 'What shall we do about it?'

And the next day they went to the police.

The police immediately told Agatha's husband, and Archie Christie arrived at the Hydro Hotel at 6.45pm on Tuesday, the 14th of December. When his wife walked out of the sitting-room, Archie saw her and went up to her.

'Hello, Agatha,' he said.

She looked at him carefully, but did not seem sure who he was. 'Hello,' she said.

* * *

The hotel was soon full of newspaper reporters.

Archie told them later, 'I don't think that my wife knows who she is. She doesn't know me, and she doesn't know where she is.'

He and Agatha left the hotel the next day. There were reporters everywhere. They followed the Christies to the railway station, trying to get pictures of the frightened Agatha, who was hiding her face behind her hands. She looked thin and her face was white.

And in London, hundreds of people were waiting at King's Cross Station for the train from Harrogate. Everyone wanted to see the 'woman of mystery' and her husband. Their lives now seemed to be like something out of one of her detective stories.

Archie helped the silent, frightened Agatha through the

crowd. Reporters shouted questions at them and took pictures, but neither Archie nor Agatha said a word.

And for the rest of her life, Agatha never again spoke about Harrogate, the Hydro Hotel, or 'Teresa Neele'. But what *really* happened that night after she left Styles? Why

The 'woman of mystery' leaving the hotel in Harrogate

did she leave her car? How did she get to Harrogate? It was always a mystery.

It still is.

CHAPTER 7

—

A young archaeologist

During the first weeks of 1927, Agatha went to stay with Madge and her husband in Cheadle, near Manchester. Archie stayed at Styles, but he wanted to marry Nancy Neele, and he asked Agatha for a divorce. At first she would not agree, but at last she said yes, and they were divorced in April 1928. Rosalind lived with Agatha.

'I don't want to use the name "Christie" again,' Agatha told her publishers. 'I will think of another name to use.'

'But you can't change it now,' they said. 'Your readers know "Agatha Christie" – that's why they buy your books. If you change your name, nobody will know who you are!'

In the end, Agatha agreed to keep the name Christie, but she was not happy about it. But William Collins was right. Thousands of people in England (and America) were reading Agatha's books now.

Then, in the autumn of 1928, Agatha decided to visit the West Indies. Rosalind was at school, and Agatha wanted a holiday in the sun, so she got tickets for a ship to Jamaica.

Two days before she left England, Agatha went to dinner with some friends. During the evening, she talked to some people who were just back from Baghdad, in Iraq. Their names were Commander and Mrs Howe.

'People always say that Baghdad is a terrible place,' said Mrs Howe. 'But we loved it.'

She went on talking about the city, and Agatha listened with great interest. She soon decided that she wanted to see Baghdad for herself.

'How do you get there?' she said. 'By sea?'

'You can go by train,' said Mrs Howe. 'On the Orient Express.'

'The Orient Express!' said Agatha. 'I've always wanted to ride on that famous train. I'll go to Baghdad, not the West Indies!'

The Howes were very helpful and wrote down the names of interesting places for Agatha to visit. 'And you must go to Ur,' Commander Howe said.

Next day, Agatha changed her tickets for the West Indies for tickets to Istanbul by the Orient Express, and then on across the desert to Baghdad.

It was an exciting journey for her, travelling alone for the first time. And later it gave her the idea for another of her most famous books – *Murder on the Orient Express*.

While she was staying in Baghdad, she remembered Commander Howe's words, 'You must go to Ur.'

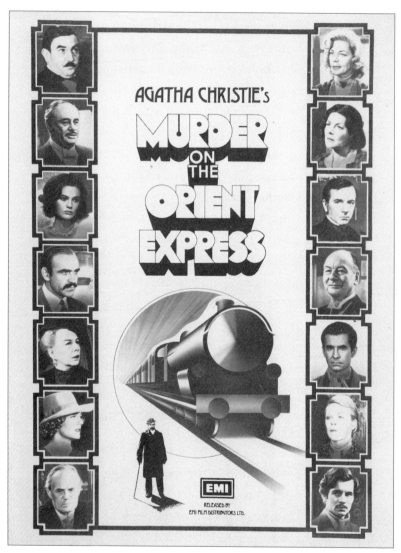

A poster for the film Murder on the Orient Express

Archaeology was something that interested Agatha very much, and Leonard Woolley, the archaeologist, and his wife were working at Ur.

Katherine Woolley was very happy to meet Agatha.

'I love your books!' she told Agatha. 'I've just finished reading *The Murder of Roger Ackroyd*. It was wonderful!'

Agatha became the Woolleys' special visitor. She loved Ur, and she loved watching the archaeologists. It was slow, tiring work, and they had to dig very carefully. Sometimes they found nothing for hours, and sometimes they found old pots or knives. It was always exciting when one of the workers found something that was thousands of years old.

'You must come back again another year,' Katherine Woolley said.

So Agatha did. She went out in March 1930, the week before the Woolleys planned to come back to England. The plan was that Agatha could travel back with them through Syria and Greece.

A young archaeologist called Max Mallowan was working with the Woolleys. He was twenty-five years old, and a quiet young man.

'I've told Max to show you Nejef and Kerbala,' Katherine Woolley told Agatha. 'Nejef is the holy city of the dead, and Kerbala has a wonderful mosque. When we leave here and go to Baghdad, he'll take you there. You can see Nippur on the way.'

'Oh, but doesn't Max want to go to Baghdad with you?' said Agatha. 'He will have friends to see there before he goes home to England.'

'Oh no,' said Katherine. 'Max will be pleased to take you.'

The young archaeologist *was* pleased to take Agatha. He liked her immediately, and Agatha liked him. They talked and laughed and enjoyed every minute of their time together.

They met the Woolleys in Baghdad, and the four of them travelled to Greece together. But when they got to their hotel in Athens, there were seven telegrams waiting for Agatha. They all said the same thing. Rosalind was ill. Agatha must come home quickly.

'I'll go with you, Agatha,' said Max.

'Oh, thank you, Max,' said Agatha. 'But haven't you got plans to——?'

'I've changed my plans,' said Max, quietly. 'I'm coming with you, Agatha.'

So they travelled home together. When they arrived, they found that Rosalind was much better, so that was one happy ending. Soon, there was another.

Agatha was fourteen years older than Max, but during the journey home Max decided to ask her an important question. And when they were back in England, he asked Agatha to marry him.

They were married on the 11th of September, 1930, in Edinburgh, in Scotland.

* * *

1930 was also the year when Agatha's other famous detective first appeared – in *The Murder at the Vicarage*. Her name was Miss Jane Marple – a little old woman who lived in the quiet English village of St Mary Mead. Miss

Max and Agatha at their home, in later years

Marple looked like somebody's grandmother, a nice kind woman who enjoyed cooking and gardening. But she also had very good eyes and ears. She saw, heard, and remembered everything – names, faces, the times of trains and buses, the colour of a shirt, the sound of a door shutting. And she always found out the name of the murderer before the police did.

Readers loved the Miss Marple stories, and she was soon as popular as Hercule Poirot. But was she a real person? Where did the idea for the character come from?

'Where? I can never remember,' Agatha always said.

Miss Jane Marple, played by the actress Margaret Rutherford

CHAPTER 8

———

Dame Agatha

For the next twenty-five years, Agatha went with Max on all his archaeological journeys. She loved travelling, and those were the happiest years of her life. It was a good time for writing, too.

'It's nice and quiet,' Agatha always said. 'There's no telephone!'

And visiting these interesting places gave her ideas for some of her best books – *Death on the Nile*, *Appointment with Death*, *Murder in Mesopotamia*, *They Came to Baghdad*. She was now one of the most popular detective-story writers in the world.

One of the many people who enjoyed her books was Queen Mary, the mother of the King of England. One day, in 1946, Agatha had a letter from the British Broadcasting Corporation in London.

'They want me to write a play for Queen Mary's 80th birthday!' she told Max. 'A play for the radio.'

'Then you must do it,' said Max.

Agatha's play for radio was called *Three Blind Mice*. Later, she wrote the play again, for a London theatre. This time it was much longer, and she gave it a new name: *The Mousetrap*.

It is a very famous play. It opened in 1952, and has been in one or other of the London theatres ever since then. In 1997, 45 years later, people were still going to see the play.

Why? It's a very good murder mystery, of course, but there is another story about *The Mousetrap*, too. Every night, at the end of the play, one of the actors talks to the people in the theatre, and says, 'Please don't tell your

First-night programme for The Mousetrap

friends who did the murder in this play. They must come to the theatre and see the play themselves!'

And everybody keeps the secret of the murderer's name – and so more and more people go to see the play.

* * *

In 1971, Queen Elizabeth made Agatha a Dame of the British Empire – a very high honour for a woman in Britain.

But why was Agatha Christie so famous? Perhaps it is because she was a wonderful story-teller. She planned her murder mysteries very carefully, putting a clue here, a clue there. And they are clever clues, so it is not easy to guess the name of the murderer. Who did it? We want to know, and by the end of the book, everything falls tidily into place – and we have the answer. And of course the stories are not really about murder and death – they are puzzles, with comfortable endings, because it is pleasing to read that the detective always catches the criminal. For an hour or two, we can escape from real life, which is often neither tidy nor comfortable.

Agatha Christie died on the 12th of January, 1976. During her life, she wrote sixty-seven detective novels, ten books of short stories, thirteen plays, six novels that were not about crime (using the name 'Mary Westmacott'), and two books about her life. Many films were made from her books; the most famous one is *Murder on the Orient Express*, made in 1974.

Today, millions of her books, in more than forty different languages, are still sold in every country of the world, from China to Nicaragua. Agatha Christie was, perhaps, the greatest detective-story writer of all time – a woman of mystery, both in books and in life.

Queen Elizabeth and Dame Agatha in 1974

GLOSSARY

agent someone who does business for another person

appear to come or go where somebody can see you

archaeology the study of very old buildings and things that are found in the ground

character a person in a story

cheat to do something that is not honest

clue a thing, or some information, that helps to find the answer to a mystery

Commander an important officer in the navy

concert music that is played or sung in front of a lot of people

desert a very hot, dry place where there is no rain (or very little)

dig (past tense **dug**) to make a hole in the ground

disappear to go where nobody can see or find you

disappointed sad, because something you wanted has not happened

dispensary a place where medicines are prepared and given to people

divorce *(n)* the end of a marriage

dream *(n)* pictures or ideas in your head when you are asleep

frightened afraid

frightening making you afraid

golf a game where a player hits a small ball into a hole with a long stick called a golf club

guess *(v)* to give an answer when you don't know if it's right or wrong

holy (city) a place (city) which is special for God

honour something very important and special

idea a new thought or plan; a picture in your head

invitation asking someone to come somewhere, or do something

lake a large piece of water with land around it

magazine a paper 'book' which comes out every week or month

maid a woman who works as a servant in a hotel
(chambermaid) or in somebody's house (housemaid)

manager someone who looks after a business (like a bank or
hotel) and tells the workers what to do

moor a large piece of wild hilly ground without trees

mosque a building where Muslims go to say their prayers

moustache the hair on a man's top lip, below his nose

novel a book that is one long story

officer someone in the army, navy, etc. who tells others what to do

play *(n)* a story that people act in the theatre

poison *(n)* something that can kill you or make you very ill if
you eat or drink it

popular if something is popular, a lot of people like it

pretty nice to look at

publish to print and make books to sell in the shops

puzzle something that is difficult to understand, like a game
where you must find an answer

railway station a place where trains stop for people to get on or
off

reporter someone who works for a newspaper, radio, or
television

return to send back, or to go back

Royal Flying Corps the first British 'army' of men to fly
aeroplanes

seem to make you think that something is true

shy not sure about yourself; finding it difficult to talk to new
people

telegram a message that is sent quickly, using radio signals

type   to use a typewriter

typewriter   a machine that you use to make letters on paper

useful   if something is useful, it helps someone to do something

volunteer   someone who does useful work but who doesn't
want any money for doing it

war   fighting between armies of different countries

Before Reading

1 Read the introduction on the first page of the book, and the back cover. How much do you know now about Agatha Christie and her books?
Tick one box for each sentence.

	YES	NO
1 Agatha Christie's books are love stories.	☐	☐
2 Her books are read all over the world.	☐	☐
3 One of her famous detectives is a woman.	☐	☐
4 Hercule Poirot is a Frenchman.	☐	☐
5 Agatha Christie had four husbands.	☐	☐
6 There are many films of her stories.	☐	☐

2 What is the mystery in Agatha Christie's life? Can you guess? Choose one of these ideas.

1 For years she lives alone in a big house and never sees or talks to anybody.
2 She helps to find a real murderer, but nobody knows how she did it.
3 She disappears for some weeks and nobody ever finds out what happened to her.
4 Somebody tries to murder her, but she never tells anybody about it.

ACTIVITIES

While Reading

Read Chapters 1 and 2, and answer these questions.

1 Why did Agatha's mother tell Agatha to write a story?
2 What happened to Agatha's first story?
3 Why did Agatha go to London when she was eighteen?
4 What did Agatha do in Cairo?
5 How did Agatha get to know Reggie Lucy?
6 Why did Agatha and Reggie have to wait before they got married?

Before you read Chapter 3, can you guess the answer to this question?

When Reggie comes home again, will Agatha marry him?

Read Chapters 3 and 4. Who said, thought, or wrote these words? Who or what were the words about?

1 'No, I don't think so. Not a *hotel*.'
2 'I've already told Reggie that I'll marry him.'
3 'Don't worry about it. I understand.'
4 'There's a war on. Who knows what will happen? Be happy while you can.'
5 'You couldn't do it. They're very difficult to do.'

6 'He'll be a very clever, very tidy little man.'

7 'Go away somewhere nice and quiet, and take it with you.'

8 'But you will need to change the last chapter.'

Read Chapters 5 and 6. Choose the best question-word for these questions, and then answer them.

What / Why

1 . . . did Agatha begin writing another book?

2 . . . was the detective Hercule Poirot like?

3 . . . did people talk about *The Murder of Roger Ackroyd*?

4 . . . did people think that Agatha disappeared?

5 . . . happened at eleven o'clock on 3rd December, 1926?

6 . . . did George Best find in a car at Newlands Corner?

7 . . . were people at the Hydro Hotel in Harrogate so interested in Mrs Teresa Neele?

8 . . . really happened on the night that Agatha Christie left Styles?

Before you read Chapters 7 and 8, can you guess which of these sentences are true?

1 Agatha and Archie decide to stay married.

2 Archie is murdered.

3 Agatha meets and marries another man.

4 Agatha spends a lot of her time travelling.

5 Agatha is famous, but unhappy, for the rest of her life.

After Reading

1 Here is a passage about Agatha Christie, but it is full of mistakes. Can you find and correct them?

Agatha Christie was a famous writer of ghost stories. She was born in 1890, was married three times, and had two sons. She met her third husband, Max Mallowan, in Scotland. He was a well-known photographer, who spent a lot of time travelling, but Agatha always stayed at home.

Agatha Christie wrote nearly two hundred books. The famous detectives in her plays are called Mr Hercule Marple and Miss Jane Poirot. Two of her best-known titles are the play *The Murder of Archie Ackroyd*, and the novel *The Mousetrap*, which you can still hear on the radio today.

2 You are a reporter in 1926, and Agatha Christie has agreed to answer five questions about her disappearance. Which questions will you ask? Choose five from the list below.

1 Why did you go away without telling anybody?
2 Were you feeling ill before you went away?
3 Did you know who you were?
4 Why did you leave your car at Newlands Corner?
5 How did you get to Harrogate?
6 Why did you choose the Hydro Hotel?

7 Why did you call yourself 'Mrs Teresa Neele'?

8 Are you in love with another man, and did you go away to meet him secretly?

9 The police thought you were dead, and your husband was the murderer. What do you say about that?

10 Your name is in every newspaper, and now more people will buy your books. Is that why you disappeared?

How did Agatha answer your five questions? Think of possible answers and write a report for the newspaper.

3 **The police ask Archie a lot of questions after Agatha disappears. Complete their conversation (use as many words as you like).**

POLICE: Were _____?

ARCHIE: No, I wasn't. I was away, staying with friends.

POLICE: And why _____?

ARCHIE: She didn't want to. She didn't know these friends.

POLICE: So did _____?

ARCHIE: She didn't say she had any plans.

POLICE: Mr Christie, where do you think _____?

ARCHIE: I don't know. I just don't know.

POLICE: Mm. Are _____?

ARCHIE: Yes. Well, er . . . we're as happy as most husbands and wives.

POLICE: I see. Tell me, Mr Christie, do _____?

ARCHIE: Yes, of course I want her to come home!

4 Find the eighteen words hidden in this word search, and draw lines through them. Words go from left to right, and from top to bottom. All the words are four letters or more, and many letters are used more than once.

M	P	U	B	L	I	S	H	E	R	U	R	D
C	H	A	P	T	E	R	E	R	S	D	P	O
H	N	D	I	V	O	R	C	E	T	E	O	M
A	T	H	P	U	Z	Z	L	E	O	T	P	A
R	D	I	S	A	P	P	E	A	R	E	U	G
A	E	G	O	N	O	V	E	L	Y	C	L	A
C	R	U	I	E	I	D	E	A	T	T	A	Z
T	N	E	M	Y	S	T	E	R	Y	I	R	I
E	T	S	E	B	O	O	K	X	P	V	P	N
R	R	S	E	S	N	C	L	U	E	E	S	E

Now write down all the letters that don't have lines through them (begin at the top and go across each line to the end). You will have twenty-four letters, which will make five words.

1 What are the five words?

2 What two things are these five words used for?

3 How is a short fat Belgian with a moustache connected with these words?

4 How did the last three of the five words begin to change Agatha Christie's life?

5 Here are titles of five Agatha Christie books. Can you match each title with one of the story descriptions below?

The Moving Finger / Death on the Nile / Murder is Easy / At Bertram's Hotel / Murder on the Orient Express

1 There have been several murders in Miss Pinkerton's village. Luke tells Miss Pinkerton that it's hard to kill a lot of people. 'The police always find out,' he says. 'Oh no,' says Miss Pinkerton, 'it's not difficult at all . . .'

2 A famous train is stopped in the snow somewhere in Europe, and a man is found murdered in his bed. One of the passengers is the murderer – but which one?

3 Hercule Poirot is on holiday in Egypt, on a boat on one of the world's most famous rivers. But one of the other passengers, Linnet Ridgeway, tells him, 'I'm afraid . . .'

4 Someone is writing unkind letters to people living in the little town of Lymstock. Who is it? But the letters are only the beginning of the mystery. Soon someone dies.

5 A train is robbed . . . someone disappears . . . someone is shot. What is going on at Miss Marple's favourite hotel?

6 What do you think about detective stories, in books or in films? Complete these sentences with your own ideas.

1 I enjoy detective stories because _____.

2 I prefer detective stories which _____.

3 I like detectives who _____.

ABOUT THE AUTHOR

John Escott worked in business before becoming a writer. Since then he has written many books for readers of all ages, but enjoys writing crime and mystery thrillers most of all. He was born in Somerset, in the west of England, but now lives in Bournemouth on the south coast. When he is not working, he likes looking for long-forgotten books in small back-street bookshops, watching old Hollywood films on video, and walking for miles along empty beaches.

He has written or retold many stories for the Oxford Bookworms Library. His original stories include *Goodbye, Mr Hollywood* (at Stage 1) and *Dead Man's Island* (at Stage 2).

OXFORD BOOKWORMS LIBRARY

Classics • Crime & Mystery • Factfiles • Fantasy & Horror
Human Interest • Playscripts • Thriller & Adventure
True Stories • World Stories

The OXFORD BOOKWORMS LIBRARY provides enjoyable reading in English, with a wide range of classic and modern fiction, non-fiction, and plays. It includes original and adapted texts in seven carefully graded language stages, which take learners from beginner to advanced level. An overview is given on the next pages.

All Stage 1 titles are available as audio recordings, as well as over eighty other titles from Starter to Stage 6. All Starters and many titles at Stages 1 to 4 are specially recommended for younger learners. Every Bookworm is illustrated, and Starters and Factfiles have full-colour illustrations.

The OXFORD BOOKWORMS LIBRARY also offers extensive support. Each book contains an introduction to the story, notes about the author, a glossary, and activities. Additional resources include tests and worksheets, and answers for these and for the activities in the books. There is advice on running a class library, using audio recordings, and the many ways of using Oxford Bookworms in reading programmes. Resource materials are available on the website <www.oup.com/bookworms>.

The *Oxford Bookworms Collection* is a series for advanced learners. It consists of volumes of short stories by well-known authors, both classic and modern. Texts are not abridged or adapted in any way, but carefully selected to be accessible to the advanced student.

You can find details and a full list of titles in the *Oxford Bookworms Library Catalogue* and *Oxford English Language Teaching Catalogues*, and on the website <www.oup.com/bookworms>.

THE OXFORD BOOKWORMS LIBRARY
GRADING AND SAMPLE EXTRACTS

STARTER • 250 HEADWORDS

present simple – present continuous – imperative –
can/cannot, must – *going to* (future) – simple gerunds …

Her phone is ringing – but where is it?

Sally gets out of bed and looks in her bag. No phone. She looks under the bed. No phone. Then she looks behind the door. There is her phone. Sally picks up her phone and answers it. *Sally's Phone*

STAGE 1 • 400 HEADWORDS

… past simple – coordination with *and*, *but*, *or* –
subordination with *before, after, when, because, so* …

I knew him in Persia. He was a famous builder and I worked with him there. For a time I was his friend, but not for long. When he came to Paris, I came after him – I wanted to watch him. He was a very clever, very dangerous man. *The Phantom of the Opera*

STAGE 2 • 700 HEADWORDS

… present perfect – *will* (future) – *(don't) have to, must not, could* –
comparison of adjectives – simple *if* clauses – past continuous –
tag questions – *ask/tell* + infinitive …

While I was writing these words in my diary, I decided what to do. I must try to escape. I shall try to get down the wall outside. The window is high above the ground, but I have to try. I shall take some of the gold with me – if I escape, perhaps it will be helpful later. *Dracula*

STAGE 3 • 1000 HEADWORDS

... should, may – present perfect continuous – *used to* – past perfect –
causative – relative clauses – indirect statements ...

Of course, it was most important that no one should see
Colin, Mary, or Dickon entering the secret garden. So Colin
gave orders to the gardeners that they must all keep away
from that part of the garden in future. *The Secret Garden*

STAGE 4 • 1400 HEADWORDS

... past perfect continuous – passive (simple forms) –
would conditional clauses – indirect questions –
relatives with *where/when* – gerunds after prepositions/phrases ...

I was glad. Now Hyde could not show his face to the world
again. If he did, every honest man in London would be proud
to report him to the police. *Dr Jekyll and Mr Hyde*

STAGE 5 • 1800 HEADWORDS

... future continuous – future perfect –
passive (modals, continuous forms) –
would have conditional clauses – modals + perfect infinitive ...

If he had spoken Estella's name, I would have hit him. I was so
angry with him, and so depressed about my future, that I could
not eat the breakfast. Instead I went straight to the old house.
Great Expectations

STAGE 6 • 2500 HEADWORDS

... passive (infinitives, gerunds) – advanced modal meanings –
clauses of concession, condition

When I stepped up to the piano, I was confident. It was as if I
knew that the prodigy side of me really did exist. And when I
started to play, I was so caught up in how lovely I looked that
I didn't worry how I would sound. *The Joy Luck Club*

The Death of Karen Silkwood

JOYCE HANNAM

This is the story of Karen Silkwood. It begins with her death.

Why does her story begin where it should end? Certain people wanted her death to be an ending. Why? What were they afraid of? Karen Silkwood had something to tell us, and she believed that it was important. Why didn't she live to tell us? Will we ever know what really happened? The questions go on and on, but there are no answers.

This is a true story. It happened in Oklahoma, USA, where Karen Silkwood lived and worked . . . and died.

The Pit and the Pendulum and Other Stories

EDGAR ALLAN POE

Retold by John Escott

Everybody has bad dreams, when horrible things move towards you in the dark, things you can hear but not see. Then you wake up, in your own warm bed, and turn over to go back to sleep.

But suppose you wake up on a hard prison floor, in a darkness blacker than the blackest night. You hear the sound of water, you touch a cold metal wall, and smell a wet dead smell. Death is all around you, waiting . . .

In these stories by Edgar Allan Poe, death whispers at you from every dark corner, and fear can drive you mad . . .